Women Inventors

Major Women in Science

MAJOR WOMEN IN SCIENCE

Women Inventors

Shaina Indovino

Mason Crest

Mason Crest
450 Parkway Drive, Suite D
Broomall, Pennsylvania 19008
www.masoncrest.com

Printed and bound in the United States of America.

First printing
9 8 7 6 5 4 3 2 1

Series ISBN: 978-1-4222-2923-1
ISBN: 978-1-4222-2932-3
ebook ISBN: 978-1-4222-8901-3

The Library of Congress has cataloged the
        hardcopy format(s) as follows:

        Library of Congress Cataloging-in-Publication Data

Indovino, Shaina Carmel.
  Women inventors / Shaina Indovino.
      pages cm. -- (Major women in science)
  Audience: Grade 7 to 8.
  Includes bibliographical references and index.
   ISBN 978-1-4222-2932-3 (hardcover) -- ISBN 978-1-4222-2923-1 (series) -- ISBN 978-1-4222-8901-3(ebook)
  1. Women inventors--Biography--Juvenile literature. 2. Inventions--History--Juvenile literature. I. Title.
  T39.I53 2014
  609.2'52--dc23
                                  2013011155

Produced by Vestal Creative Services.
www.vestalcreative.com

Contents

Introduction

Have you wondered about how the natural world works? Are you curious about how science could help sick people get better? Do you want to learn more about our planet and universe? Are you excited to use technology to learn and share ideas? Do you want to build something new?

Scientists, engineers, and doctors are among the many types of people who think deeply about science and nature, who often have new ideas on how to improve life in our world.

We live in a remarkable time in human history. The level of understanding and rate of progress in science and technology have never been greater. Major advances in these areas include the following:

- Computer scientists and engineers are building mobile and Internet technology to help people access and share information at incredible speeds.
- Biologists and chemists are creating medicines that can target and get rid of harmful cancer cells in the body.
- Engineers are guiding robots on Mars to explore the history of water on that planet.
- Physicists are using math and experiments to estimate the age of the universe to be greater than 13 billion years old.
- Scientists and engineers are building hybrid cars that can be better for our environment.

Scientists are interested in discovering and understanding key principles in nature, including biological, chemical, mathematical, and physical aspects of our world. Scientists observe, measure, and experiment in a systematic way in order to test and improve their understanding. Engineers focus on applying scientific knowledge and math to find creative solutions for technical problems and to develop real products for people to use. There are many types of engineering, including computer, electrical, mechanical, civil, chemical, and biomedical engineering. Some people have also found that studying science or engineering can help them succeed in other professions such as law, business, and medicine.

Both women and men can be successful in science and engineering. This book series highlights women leaders who have made significant contributions across many scientific fields, including chemistry, medicine, anthropology, engineering, and physics. Historically, women have faced barriers to training and building careers in science, which makes some of these stories even more amazing. While not all barriers have been overcome, our society has made tremendous progress in educating and advancing women in science. Today, there are schools, organizations, and resources to enable women to pursue careers as scientists or engineers at the highest levels of achievement and leadership.

The goals of this series are to help you:

1. Learn about women scientists, engineers, doctors, and inventors who have made a major impact in science and our society
2. Understand different types of science and engineering
3. Explore science and math in school and real life

You can do a lot of things to learn more about science, math, and engineering. Explore topics in books or online, take a class at school, go to science camp, or do experiments at home. More important, talk to a real scientist! Call or e-mail your local college to find students and professors. They would love to meet with you. Ask your doctors about their education and training. Or you can check out these helpful resources:

- *Nova* has very cool videos about science, including profiles on real-life women scientists and engineers: www.pbs.org/wgbh/nova.
- *National Geographic* has excellent photos and stories to inspire people to care about the planet: science.nationalgeographic.com/science.
- Here are examples of online courses for students, of which many are free to use:
  1. Massachusetts Institute of Technology (MIT) OpenCourseWare highlights for high school: ocw.mit.edu/high-school.
  2. Khan Academy tutorials and courses: www.khanacademy.org.
  3. Stanford University Online, featuring video courses and programs for middle and high school students: online.stanford.edu.

Other skills will become important as you get older. Build strong communication skills, such as asking questions and sharing your ideas in class. Ask for advice or help when needed from your teachers, mentors, tutors, or classmates. Be curious and resilient: learn from your successes and mistakes. The best scientists do.

Learning science and math is one of the most important things that you can do in school. Knowledge and experience in these areas will teach you how to think and how the world works and can provide you with many adventures and paths in life. I hope you will explore science—you could make a difference in this world.

Ann Lee-Karlon, PhD
President
Association for Women in Science
San Francisco, California

1

What Does It Take to Be an Inventor?

Have you ever looked at a piece of **technology** and thought about how you could make it better? Or have you ever seen a problem in daily life and found yourself building a solution to it in your head? If so, then you just might be an inventor!

Inventors are people who come up with new ideas—and then turn those ideas into reality. They create brand-new things that have never existed before or totally different ways of doing something. They look for ways to solve problems and improve on existing ideas to develop a useful item that fills a need. Some have changed the way the entire world lives!

Think about it. Agriculture was invented by someone. Without farming, human beings would not have been able to settle down and build societies. Could you imagine what it would be like if we were still a group of hunters and gatherers? Or what about the wheel? Imagine what the world would be like if no one had ever come up with this simple but powerful invention!

Think about what you do on a daily basis. The food you eat, the house where you live, and even the bus you ride to school are all **complex** inventions. But these inventions were not always this complicated. An invention that has been around for a long time can always be added to or improved. Without the internal combustion engine, for example, the school bus would never have been developed. Even very old inventions like the wheel continue to be improved; today, scientists are still looking for ways to make better tires. New inventions are always being created—inventors will never be out of a job!

Not all inventors are scientists. Some inventors are simply good at solving problems and coming up with new ideas. However, many inventors do have scientific backgrounds.

Why Be an Inventor?

Inventors change the world. They save people time by developing labor-saving devices (like vacuum cleaners and power lawn mowers). They create new ways of communicating—like the telephone and the Internet—linking people all around the world. Sometimes they make the world a safer place; the invention of seatbelts, for example, makes riding in a car much safer, and modern medicine helps most of us survive to a ripe, old age. Just a few centuries ago, the life expectancy of a human being was around forty or fifty years, while today, thanks to countless modern inventions, most people in the developed world live past seventy!

Many inventions simply make life easier in some way. Computers, for example, make typing, calculating, and solving problems far faster and easier. Eyeglasses allow people with poor vision to see well. Waterproof boots let us walk through the rain or snow without getting our feet wet.

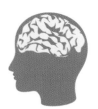

Although better known for being an actress, Hedy Lamarr was also an inventor in the field of wireless communications. She helped develop a "Secret Communications System" to help combat the Nazis in World War II. By manipulating radio frequencies at irregular intervals between transmission and reception, the invention formed an unbreakable code to prevent classified messages from being intercepted by the enemy.

Inventions can be big or little. Computers and the Internet have **revolutionized** the way people live. But waterproof boots are pretty important too, especially if you live where it is often raining or snowing!

Education

Being an inventor doesn't require any formal education. In fact, some of the inventors in this book already came up with their first big inventions by the age of twelve! Education, however, can help you learn how to think creatively. The more you understand about how the world works, the better you'll be able to think of ways to improve it.

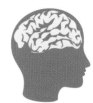

Ten Steps to Becoming an Inventor

1. Make a habit of wondering how things work—and then imagining how they could be taken just one step farther to work a little better. Think outside the box!

2. Keep a notebook where you write down your observations and ideas. Make sketches. Go back and look at old ideas and sketches regularly, to see if something new has occurred to you.

3. With your parents' permission, take things apart to see how they work. With words and sketches, keep a record in your notebook of what things look like before you take them apart—and then put them back together.

4. Learn how to repair broken things—TVs, computers, can openers, bikes; anything and everything! The more you know how to repair something, the more you'll understand about how it works.

5. Think about whether you could improve any of the things you've taken apart and repaired. Make more notes and sketches in your notebooks.

6. Look over your ideas. Ask yourself:
   • Would any of my ideas make life easier for people in some way?
   • Do a lot of people need or want any of my ideas?
   • Is it possible for me to turn any of my ideas into a reality?
   • What would I need to build it (money, materials, tools, etc.)?

7. Get to work and make a plan! Your plan should include:
   • detailed sketches
   • tools you will need
   • materials you will need
   • a budget that will cover both materials and tools
   • the place where you will build it (your garage, for example, or your basement)
   • a schedule with goals to be achieved at various intervals (for example, at the end of the first week, you will have so much done; at the end of the second week, you will have reached another milestone). Keep your goals realistic.

8. Put your plan into action. Make your invention!

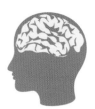

9. Test your invention. Does it work as planned? Does it have problems? If so, fine-tune your invention until you're satisfied with the way it works.

10. Share your invention with the world! This may mean giving it away to your friends and family—or it could mean selling it to people who are eager for this brand-new thing you've made.

You probably won't find "inventor" as a job listed in the want ads either. Many inventors must first develop their ideas using their own money, on their own time. Then, if they're successful at creating something new and useful that people want to buy, they can make money by selling their invention.

However, many companies do have "research-and-development" departments (often referred to as "R&D"). R&D departments develop new products, processes, and services for the company to sell. Companies hire people to work in their R&D departments, so these inventors get a regular paycheck. If a person comes up with a successful new product, she may be named as an inventor on a company's patent and the company will own the right to make, use, or sell the product.

R&D jobs are usually scientific in nature. They could be in the field of computer science, chemistry, biology, engineering, or some other scientific field. To get one of these jobs, you'll probably need a master's degree and possibly a PhD. This could take you two to ten years after graduation from a four-year college.

Character

All inventors are very creative. But it takes more than just creativity to succeed as an inventor.

Unfortunately, something new does not always work right the first time. An inventor might experience problems she could have never imagined when she was creating her first **prototype**. If she's easily discouraged, her great new idea will never see the light of the day; it will end up shoved in the back of a closet somewhere and forgotten. Successful inventors have to be patient and determined. They have to be able to learn from their mistakes and keep going.

Earl Corl, the president of Idea Buyer, a product-development company, lists these traits as essential to every inventor:

1. **A bias toward action.** By this he means that when inventors see a problem, they are more inclined to do something than to sit around doing nothing. When an opportunity presents itself, they move quickly and intelligently to make use of it—and when a problem arises, they are able to act just as quickly to deal with it so that it creates the least amount of damage. They don't wait around for answers to show up. Instead, they act and find those answers.

2. **Decisiveness.** Inventors can't be wishy-washy. They have to be able to make up their minds, so that they can act.

3. **Integrity.** Corl says that integrity is vital to inventors' success because people need to know they can trust them not to take shortcuts or falsify their results.

4. **Focus.** People who are focused devote the most time to the things that move their goals closer to realization. Successful inventors know that every second they spend on other things is time they aren't spending on finishing, packaging, and marketing their product.

5. **Loyalty to your goals.** Inventors are often faced with seemingly better opportunities. Instead of switching goals, however, successful inventors stick with their original goals until they're achieved. They follow through.

6. **A strong sense of why you're doing what you're doing.** Successful inventors know the answers to these two questions: Why are you an inventor? And why are you inventing what you are inventing? One of the main reasons inventors don't reach their goals, according to Corl, is because they never had good reasons for setting them in the first place. Maybe they just wanted to impress their friends or family. Maybe they wanted to get rich quickly. Successful inventors are passionate about what they're doing—and they're totally convinced that their inventions are necessary additions to the world.

Do you have these traits? If you don't have them now, do you think you could develop them? If so, you might be like one of the creative and resourceful women inventors who helped to change our world.

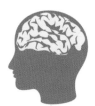

Words to Know

Technology: the machinery and tools created using scientific knowledge.
Complex: having many different and connected parts.
Revolutionized: changed dramatically.
Prototype: the first model of something, from which other forms are copied.

Find Out More

Braun, Sandra. *Incredible Women Inventors*. Toronto, Ont.: Second Story, 2007.

Casey, Susan. *Kids Inventing: A Handbook for Young Inventors*. Hoboken, N.J.: John Wiley, 2005.

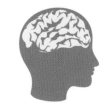

2

Amanda Theodosia Jones:

Better Ways to Preserve Food

Amanda Theodosia Jones is known for her creation of a canning process and an oil burner. However, she was also a woman of many other talents. She was a teacher, writer, and editor before becoming an inventor. Amanda was also very outspoken about women's rights. She even demanded that her canning business be run completely by women.

Amanda was born on October 19, 1835, in East Bloomfield, New York. She came from a large family, the fourth child of twelve brothers and sisters. An intelligent girl, she was interested in everything around her—and she enjoyed teaching others about the world as well. In fact, Amanda became a teacher when

A Business for Women

Amanda was very passionate about women in the workplace. She believed strongly in a woman's right to have the same privileges as men. In 1890, she started a canning company based on her method of vacuum-sealing canned foods. Rather than hiring men, Amanda believed that only woman should run her company. She said, "This is a woman's industry. No man will vote our stock, transact our business, pronounce on women's wages, supervise our factories. Give men whatever work is suitable, but keep the governing power [for women]."

she was only fifteen! She also loved to write poetry and literature, some of which was published.

Amanda had lots of health problems, but she managed to overcome them. As a young adult, she moved to Chicago and became an editor for a magazine.

By this time, scientists had realized that when air touches food, the food spoils faster. Air allows bacteria and mold to grow, which can make humans very sick when it is eaten. By Amanda's day, food was being stored in glass jars—but the food inside the jars often spoiled.

Amanda was aware of this problem—and she thought of a way to fix it. She realized that if the air could somehow be removed from the jars, food would last a lot longer. In 1872, she invented a mechanism to remove as much air as possible from food while it was being jarred. In order to do this, hot liquid was put into the jar right before it was sealed, forming a **vacuum**. After this process, no air was left, and no bacteria or mold could grow inside the preserved food. Her invention was named the Jones Process after her last name. Amanda received several patents for her process of vacuum sealing various kinds of foods, including wet foods, dry foods, dehydrated foods, and liquids.

Because of Amanda, foods could now be **preserved** longer. They could be shipped across the country and around the world. Amanda's invention was not only very helpful in her day, though—it is still used today. Canned foods are still made using Amanda's vacuum process.

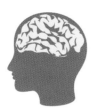

What Is a Patent?

A patent is a property right for an invention that is granted by a government to the inventor. A United States patent gives inventors the right "to exclude others from making, using, offering for sale, or selling their invention throughout the United States or importing their invention into the United States" for a limited period of time. The patent makes sure that no one else can claim credit for an invention besides the inventor—and that no one else can sell it either.

This wasn't Amanda's only invention. She also worked on a heating furnace that burned oil for heat. Unlike firewood, oil could keep an area warm for longer. For people living in cold areas, the oil burner truly changed their way of life. She received a patent for this invention in 1880.

Throughout her life, Amanda suffered many illnesses, but she continued to publish works until her death in 1914. She was twice listed in "Who's Who in America," and she obtained twelve patents during her lifetime. Today, she is remembered as an intelligent and creative female inventor who helped to change the way food is processed—an invention that helped to change the way we live.

Words to Know

Vacuum: a space that does not contain any matter.
Preserved: kept in an original state.

Find Out More

Blashfield, Jean F. *Women Inventors*. Minneapolis, Minn.: Capstone, 2007.

Cefrey, Holly. *The Inventions of Amanda Jones: The Vacuum Method of Canning and Food Preservation*. New York: PowerKids, 2003.

Femilogue, "Amanda Theodosia Jones"
femilogue.blogspot.com/2012/10/amanda-theodosia-jones.html

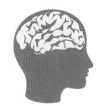

3

Margaret Knight:

Paperbag Inventor

Inventors have a natural curiosity about the world, and they are always looking for ways to improve it. Margaret Knight was a problem solver who made her first invention at the age of only twelve. By the time of her death, she was a well-respected inventor who held over eighty patents! Some of Margaret's inventions are still used in some form today.

Margaret Knight was born on February 14, 1838, in York, Maine. When she was a little girl, her father died, leaving Margaret's mother to raise her children alone. To help support her family, Margaret had to start working when she was still a child. She worked in a cotton mill from the time she was twelve until she was in her fifties.

While she was working in the textile mill, Margaret watched as something went wrong with one of the machines. A piece of thread got caught in a type of sewing machine, which caused a **spindle** to fly off and hit someone nearby. A flying spindle traveling at a high speed could really hurt someone! Margaret's mind started working the way a good inventor's works: she started thinking of ways to keep spindles from flying off like that.

Who Was the First Woman to Receive a U.S. Patent?

The first was Hannah Wilkinson Slater, wife of industrialist Samuel Slater. She invented two-ply thread, becoming in 1793 the first American woman to be granted a patent.

Her solution was to find a way to force the machine to immediately stop when anything became caught in it. Margaret's idea was simple but effective. It prevented many accidents. And she was only twelve years old!

Throughout her entire life, Margaret was always finding new ways to improve the world. One of her most famous inventions is something we still use today. Every time you go to the grocery store and use a paper bag, you use one of Margaret's inventions.

Margaret invented a wooden machine that folded and glued paper bags. The paper bags being created at the time didn't have flat bottoms. Instead, they were

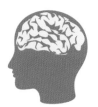

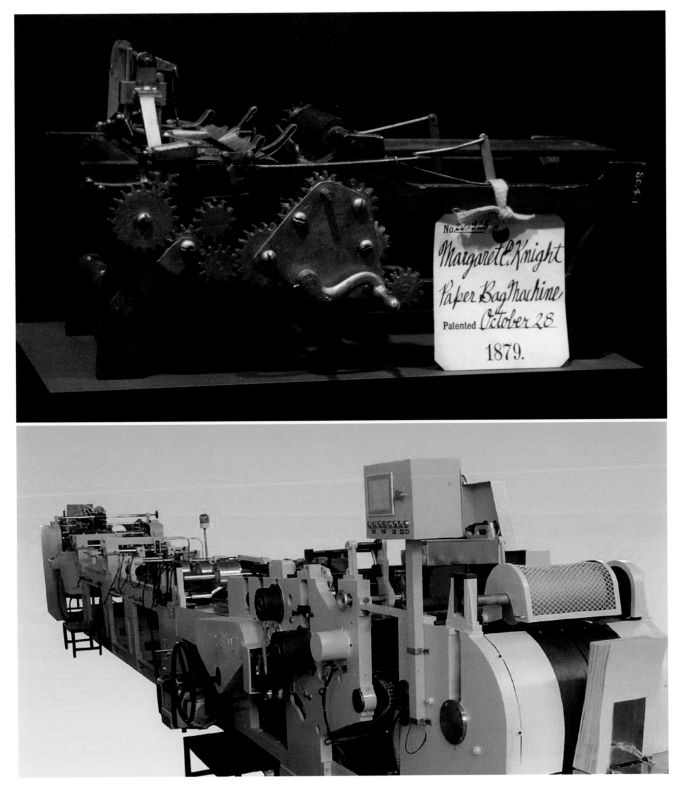

Modern paper bag machinery (bottom) is bigger and more complicated than Margaret's (top), but it is uses the same ideas that she devised to make a flat-bottomed paper bag.

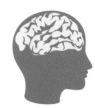

shaped more like envelopes, which made it difficult to store a lot of items inside them. Margaret realized that bags with flat bottoms would be much better. Margaret came up with the idea of making paper bags with flat rectangular bottoms and tall sides.

Margaret invented a machine that folded and glued the paper to form the flat-bottomed brown paper bags familiar to shoppers today. She first built a wooden model of the device, but she needed a working iron model to apply for a patent.

But then Margaret ran into trouble. A man who was in the machine shop where her iron model was being built stole her design and patented the device in his name. But Margaret didn't back down. She filed a **lawsuit** against the man—and she won. She proved to the court that the idea was really hers, and she was awarded the patent in 1871. She was the second woman to ever receive an American patent. Then, with a Massachusetts businessman, Margaret formed the Eastern Paper Bag Company. Now she could begin to sell her great new idea.

Margaret didn't stop thinking of new ideas. She invented a numbering machine, a new type of window frame and sash, and several devices to improve the **rotary** engine. When Margaret died in 1914, at the age of seventy-six, she had received eighty-seven patents. Today, her original bag-making machine is in the Smithsonian Museum in Washington, D.C. In 2006, she was **inducted** in the National Inventors Hall of Fame. Her **ingenuity** and drive has never been forgotten.

Words to Know

Spindle: a rod used in spinning thread by hand.

Lawsuit: a conflict brought to a court of law for a judge and possibly a jury to decide.

Rotary: characterized by moving around a center point in a circle.

Inducted: formally welcomed into an organization.

Ingenuity: cleverness and inventiveness.

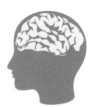

Find Out More

Famous Women Inventors, "Margaret Knight"
www.women-inventors.com/Margaret-Knight.asp

Kulling, Monica, and David Parkins. *In the Bag! Margaret Knight Wraps It Up.* Toronto: Tundra, 2011.

McCully, Emily Arnold. *Marvelous Mattie: How Margaret E. Knight Became an Inventor.* New York: Farrar, Straus and Giroux, 2006.

National Women's History Museum, "Margaret E. Knight (1838–1914)"
www.nwhm.org/education-resources/biography/biographies/margaret-knight/

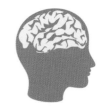

4

Mary Anderson: Windshield Wiper Inventor

Imagine you're riding down the road in a car during a heavy snowstorm—but the car doesn't have any windshield wipers! The snow just keeps building up on the glass. You have to keep stopping to wipe off your windshield so you can see to drive. At times, you stick your head out the side window and try to see the road. You're scared you're going to drive into a ditch or hit something. If a police officer comes along, you might even get a ticket. It's against the law today to drive without windshield wipers. Before Mary Anderson came up with her bright idea, though, there were no windshield wipers.

Mary was born in 1866 in Green County, Alabama. When she was a young woman, she, her mother, and her sister moved from the country to the big city of Birmingham, Alabama. There, Mary built an apartment building and started collecting rents. She was already an **enterprising** young woman!

In 1893, Mary moved to California. There she operated a cattle ranch and a vineyard. Women in the nineteenth century were expected to marry and raise a family—but Mary refused to be confined to those roles. She proved that women have the intelligence and drive to be successful businesspeople.

Around the turn of the century, Mary took a trip to New York City. There she noticed that streetcar drivers had to open the windows of their cars whenever it rained in order to see. Mary thought about the problem and came up with a good idea. She built a swinging arm device with a rubber blade that the driver could operate with a lever from inside the vehicle.

Another Woman Inventor

Mary Anderson's windshield wiper had to be operated by hand with a lever. But another woman improved on her idea. Charlotte Bridgwood received the patent for the automatic windshield wiper in 1917.

Mary got a patent for her idea in 1903, but at first, people were leery of her invention. They thought those blades swinging back and forth on the windshield might distract drivers. By 1916, though, almost all cars came from the factory with windshield wipers built in.

Mary Anderson died in 1953 at the age of eighty-seven. She is remembered as an intelligent woman with a true inventor's spirit. When she saw a problem, she found a way to fix it!

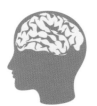

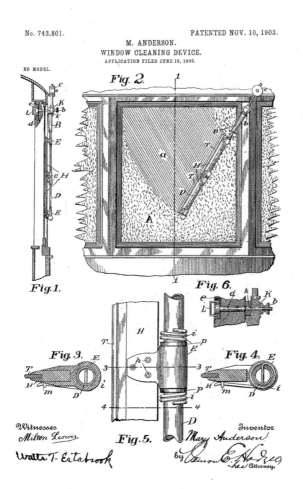

The drawing of Mary's invention, which accompanied her patent application. Mary's signature appears at the bottom.

Words to Know
Enterprising: showing initiative and responsibility.

Find Out More
Famous Women Inventors, "Mary Anderson"
www.women-inventors.com/Mary-Anderson.asp

Moxie Magazine, "Mary Anderson, Southern Bell"
www.moxiemag.com/moxie/articles/profiles/maryand.html

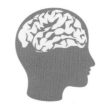

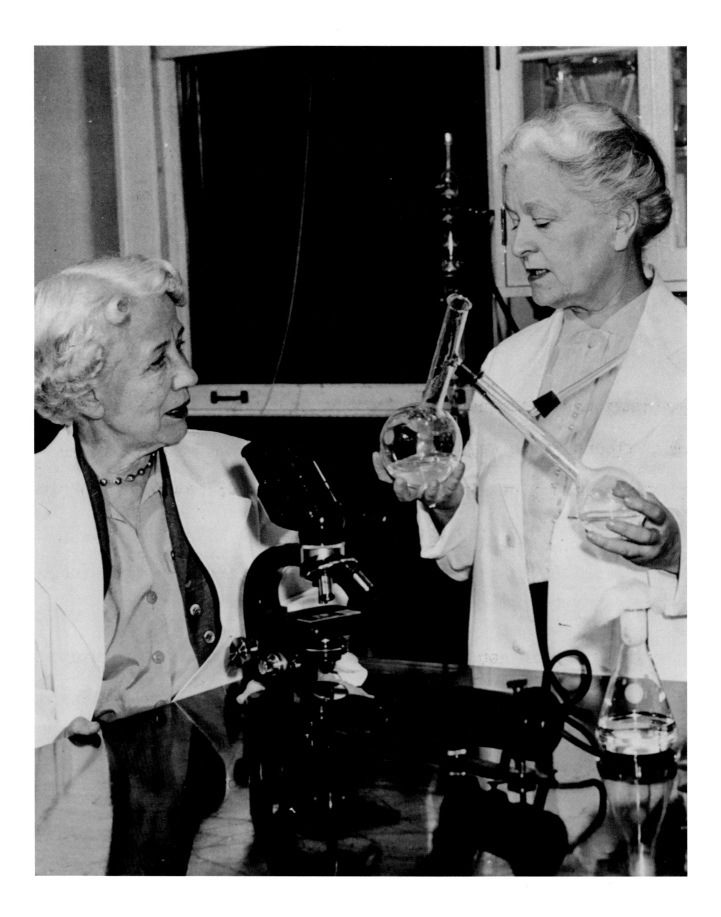

5

Elizabeth Lee Hazen and Rachel Fuller Brown:

Nystatin Inventors

Not all inventors work alone. Sometimes they work in teams. This is what Rachel Fuller Brown and Elizabeth Lee Hazen did. Together, they invented a type of medicine known as Nystatin. Their invention saved the lives of many people.

The world is full of different kinds of **fungi**. Some of these can be dangerous to humans. They can get inside our bodies and make us sick. Healthy people can usually fight off a fungal infection without any problem, but people with

Dealing with Side Effects

Sometimes a new invention causes unforeseen problems. Today we take for granted the antibiotics doctors often prescribe when we have an infection. But the first antibiotic, penicillin, wasn't discovered until 1928. In the years that followed, antibiotics were used more and more to fight bacterial illnesses. Antibiotics saved lives, but they had a side effect too—when the antibiotics killed the disease-causing bacteria, they also killed the healthy bacteria the human body needs. Healthy bacteria ate the fungus that would otherwise grow inside the human body. Without that bacteria, fungus grew inside people's bodies. Fungal infections cause sore throats and upset stomachs. They cause athlete's foot and ringworm. They could also cause serious infections that attack the central nervous system. Doctors and scientists didn't understand fungal diseases—and when Elizabeth and Rachel started working together, there were no antifungal medications that were safe for human use.

weakened **immune systems** cannot fight off infections as easily. Today, modern medicine gives these people extra help—but before Elizabeth Hazen and Rachel Brown, no such medicine existed.

Elizabeth Lee Hazen was born on August 24, 1885, in Mississippi. Her early childhood was difficult because her parents died when she was only four years old. An aunt and uncle adopted Elizabeth and her siblings, though, and she grew up to graduate with a bachelor's degree from the Mississippi University for Women.

Elizabeth then taught high school biology and physics in Jackson, Mississippi, while she continued her education by attending summer school at the University of Tennessee and the University of Virginia. Eventually, she was accepted into Columbia's biology department for graduate studies. She completed a master's degree in 1917 and a PhD in **microbiology** in 1927. She was one of Columbia's first female doctoral students.

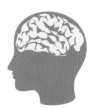

While she studied, Elizabeth had also been working. During World War I, she worked in the Army's **diagnostic** laboratory, and in the 1920s, she worked with a drug called Ricin that came from the castor oil plant. Although Ricin is very poisonous, it can also be used as a medicine. Elizabeth was researching its effect on the bacteria that causes botulism. (Botulism is a very dangerous disease caused by a bacteria getting into food.)

Elizabeth continued her research in bacteria and **immunology**. Then in 1931, she was offered a job working with the New York State Department of Health. She accepted and worked in the Bacterial Diagnosis Laboratory Division in New York City. She had several major accomplishments there: she traced an outbreak of **anthrax**, she located sources of a disease called tularemia, and she traced the source of food poisoning from improperly preserved foods. Elizabeth had an inquiring mind—and she knew how to keep working until she found answers.

Elizabeth moved next into a job at the New York City office of the Division of Laboratories and Research of the State Department of Public Health. There she studied more about fungi and fungal diseases. Then, in 1944, the head of Elizabeth's division chose her to head up an investigation into fungi and its relation to bacteria and other **microbes**. The project needed more than a microbiologist; it also needed a **biochemist**. The division chose Rachel Fuller Brown to work with her.

Rachel Fuller Brown had been born on November 23, 1898, in Springfield, Massachusetts. The family later moved to Missouri, but when Rachel was fourteen, her father left the family.

Money was scarce. Rachel's family moved back to Springfield, where Rachel enrolled in a commercial high school, a special school that prepared students for business. Rachel already had ideas about how she could help her family—but her mother forced her to transfer to the regular high school for a more traditional education.

Rachel worked hard at her studies. Her determination impressed a friend of her grandmother's so much that the friend decided to pay for Rachel to attend Mount Holyoke College. At first, Rachel planned to major in history, but she also fell in love with chemistry. In 1920, she earned her bachelor's degree in both chemistry and history.

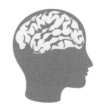

After working as a **laboratory assistant** for a while, Rachel eventually went back to school and got her master's degree in **organic chemistry** from the University of Chicago in 1921. She then taught for three years at a girls' school and college in Chicago.

Finally, Rachel was able to return to the University of Chicago for additional graduate work in organic chemistry and **bacteriology**. By 1926, she had completed her research project and all the required course work, as well as her PhD **thesis**.

But then she ran out of money. Rachel needed to get a job. She left Chicago without taking her oral exams for her PhD and went to work at the Division of Labor and Research in Albany, New York.

The Division of Labor and Research, another major branch of the New York State Department of Health, was famous for its research into human diseases and its invention of vaccines. Rachel worked there for seven years without her PhD. Finally, when she had an opportunity to go back to Chicago for a scientific meeting, she arranged to take her oral examinations at last. Now she finally had her PhD!

At work, Rachel focused on identifying the types of bacteria that caused pneumonia. She helped develop a pneumonia **vaccine** that is still used today. She also worked on ways to improve the test for syphilis (a sexually transmitted infection).

During the 1940s, the New York State Department of Health was very worried about fungal infections. These diseases were often deadly, and doctors had no way to fight these diseases. This was the project that finally brought Elizabeth and Rachel together.

Even though the two women worked for the same organization and on the same project, the laboratories they worked in were far apart. Elizabeth was in New York City, and Rachel was 150 miles away in Albany. Rachel and Elizabeth's partnership would never have worked if it weren't for the United States Postal Service.

Their research needed to be done in several steps. First, Elizabeth would combine **microorganisms** and fungi. The microorganisms she used were found in different soil samples, which were sent to her lab from all over the world. If the microorganisms in the soil killed the fungi, she would put a sample in a glass jar and mail it to Rachel in Albany.

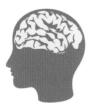

Rachel's job was to figure out what ingredient in the soil sample had killed the fungi. Once she had, she sent the sample back to Elizabeth. Now, Elizabeth had to see if it was safe to use. Nearly all the samples that killed the test fungi also turned out to be very poisonous to animals. This meant they weren't safe for people either.

A Powerful New Medicine

Nystatin not only cured many serious fungal infections of the skin, mouth, throat, and intestinal tract, but it could also be combined with antibacterial drugs to balance their side effects. Over the years, Nystatin has proved to be good for other things as well as fighting human diseases. For example, it stopped fungal growth on flood-damaged works of art in Florence, Italy, and it helped to slow the spread of disease that was killing elm trees in the United States.

And then a lucky coincidence happened. Rachel and Elizabeth had been looking at soil samples from around the world. Out of the hundreds of samples they had examined, the one that finally worked—and was not fatal to animals—came from soil on the property of one of Elizabeth's friends. Elizabeth was so excited that she named the microorganism after her friends!

Rachel and Elizabeth weren't done yet. They needed to do more chemical work. They needed to make sure the microorganism was safe for human use. Eventually, though, they had done it: they had invented a drug that would kill fungi. They named it "Nystatin," in honor of the New York State Division of Laboratories and Research where they both worked.

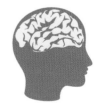

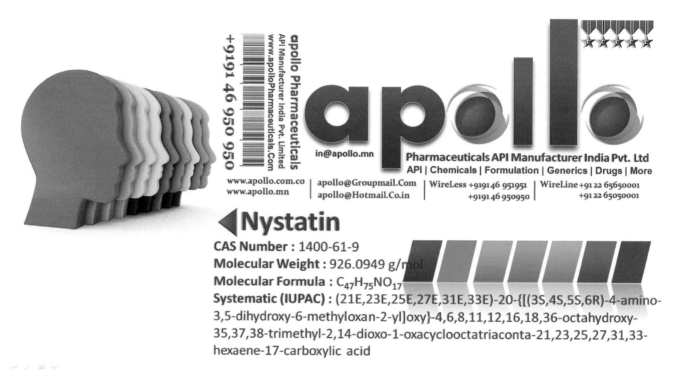

◀ Nystatin

CAS Number : 1400-61-9
Molecular Weight : 926.0949 g/mol
Molecular Formula : $C_{47}H_{75}NO_{17}$
Systematic (IUPAC) : (21E,23E,25E,27E,31E,33E)-20-{[(3S,4S,5S,6R)-4-amino-3,5-dihydroxy-6-methyloxan-2-yl]oxy}-4,6,8,11,12,16,18,36-octahydroxy-35,37,38-trimethyl-2,14-dioxo-1-oxacyclooctatriaconta-21,23,25,27,31,33-hexaene-17-carboxylic acid

Today, Nystatin is sold all around the world. Babies and AIDS patients are just some of the people whose lives are improved by Rachel and Elizabeth's invention.

Rachel and Elizabeth continued to work together in the years that followed. Together they discovered two antibiotics. They also made other contributions to the field of bacteriology over the years, until they both retired from their work. Elizabeth died in 1975, and Rachel died in 1980.

During their lifetimes, they refused to use any money Nystatin earned to make themselves rich. Instead, the $13.4 million went to a **trust fund** they managed. The money was used to support scientific research and to help other women advance in the field of science. Shortly before her death, Rachel said, "I hope for a future of equal opportunities and accomplishments for all scientists regardless of sex."

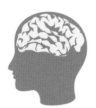

Words to Know

Fungi: a type of organism that includes mushrooms, yeast, and mold.

Immune systems: the parts of the human body that fight off invasions of bacteria, viruses, and other infections.

Microbiology: the study of tiny organisms like fungi and bacteria.

Diagnostic: concerned with identifying illnesses.

Immunology: the branch of medicine that studies the immune system.

Anthrax: a disease of the skin and lungs caused by bacteria often carried by sheep and cows.

Microbes: tiny, disease-causing organisms.

Biochemist: a scientist who studies the chemical makeup of living things.

Laboratory assistant: a person trained to perform tasks in a room used to conduct scientific experiments.

Organic chemistry: the study of substances containing carbon, which is found in all living things.

Bacteriology: the study of bacteria, a type of tiny organism.

Thesis: a large project to complete at the end of a master's or PhD degree.

Vaccines: medicines used to provide protection from specific diseases.

Microorganisms: a type of tiny organism, such as bacteria and fungi.

Trust fund: money to be inherited in the future.

Find Out More

Invent Now, "HALL OF FAME / inventor profile: Elizabeth Lee Hazen"
www.invent.org/hall_of_fame/75.html

Invent Now, "HALL OF FAME / inventor profile: Rachel Fuller Brown"
www.invent.org/hall_of_fame/20.html

Wayne, Tiffany K. *American Women of Science Since 1900.* Santa Barbara, Calif.: ABC-CLIO, 2010.

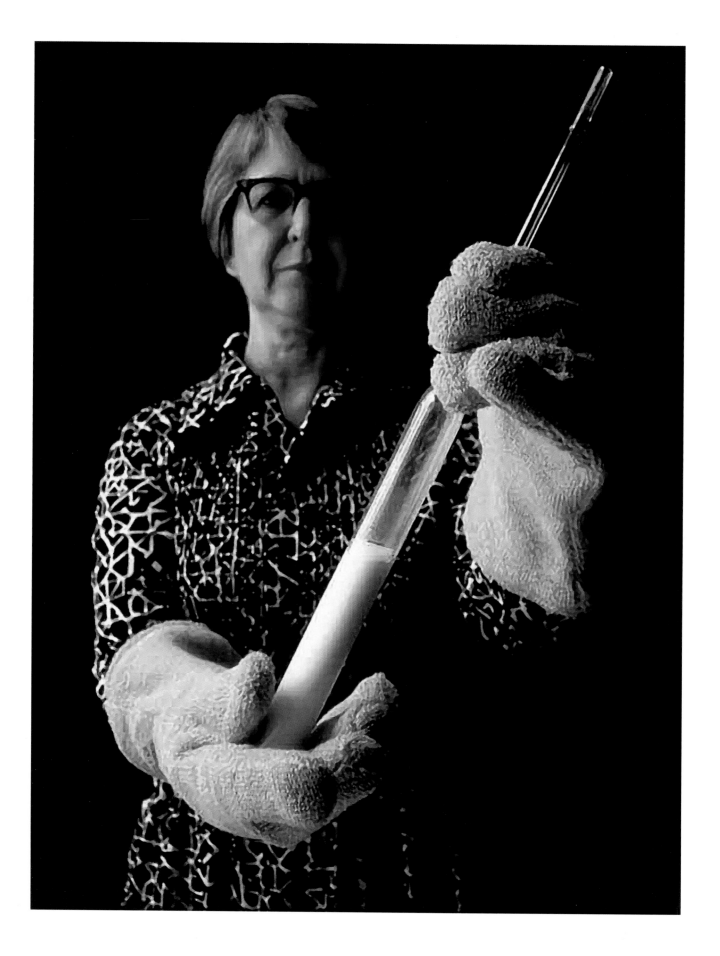

6

Stephanie Kwolek:

Inventor of Body Armor

I magine you're a chemist working in a research laboratory. Your boss has asked you to find a new way to create fibers that can be used in fabrics. You spend some of your time experimenting with the chemical compounds you and your coworkers have already made. At other times, you heat, stir, and spin new substances to see what you can create. Because you studied chemistry in college, and because you have been working in a laboratory for a few years, you know what you're doing—and you're having fun.

One day, you're going through the same routines when something strange happens. The mixture you're working with turns cloudy instead of clear. When you stir it, the glop doesn't look the way you expect. You turn around and shout to the other people working in your lab, "Hey! Something really cool is happening!" They all gather around you and watch while you run some tests on this mysterious substance.

Did You Know?

A vest made out of seven layers of aramid fibers weighs 2.5 pounds—but it can stop a knife blade as well as a .38-caliber bullet shot from 10 feet away.

It turns out you've invented a brand-new substance that can be used in fabrics. It weighs very little—but it's stiff and stronger than anyone could have ever imagined. Not so good for creating a new pair of jeans or children's pajamas—but really, really useful, it turns out, for protecting police officers from bullets.

You're invention ends up being used to make bullet-resistant vests and helmets. You've invented something that will save thousands of lives. Not a bad day's work!

This is the real-life story of Stephanie Kwolek, who was born on July 31, 1923 in Pennsylvania. As a young girl, she enjoyed exploring nature with her father which led to her interest in science. When Stephanie was only ten years old, though, her father died. Now, it was her mother's turn to teach Stephanie about fabrics and sewing.

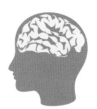

"I did not start out to be a chemist," Stephanie said. "As a child, I thought that I might be a fashion designer. I spent an awful lot of time drawing various types of clothes and sewing." In school, however, Stephanie enjoyed her science and math classes, and her teachers encouraged her, helping her be a good student and talking to her about careers in science and chemistry. In high school, she decided she wanted to have a career in medicine. "I was always interested in science and mathematics," she said. "It was only natural I would go into some form of science."

As was common in those days, Stephanie went to a women's college that was part of a much larger, all-men's university. (Today, the two colleges are both part of the co-ed Carnegie Mellon University.) Her fellow students and professors were all women who were interested in science, which encouraged her to stick with her interest in science. She majored in chemistry, with the plan that she would go on to medical school after she graduated.

But first she had to earn enough money to pay for graduate school. She interviewed for jobs at several research companies, including the DuPont company. The person who interviewed her at DuPont told her he would let her know in a few weeks if she got the job. "I decided to be very bold," Stephanie said, "and I said, 'I wonder if you could tell me sooner, because I have some companies requesting that I give them an answer whether I will accept their offers or not.' And this was true!" The man offered her the job then and there!

Stephanie loved her new job in the textile lab. "The first year, the work was so interesting and it was so challenging," she said. "I loved to solve problems, and it was a constant learning process. Each day there was something new, a new challenge, and I loved that."

In fact, she got so interested in chemistry and research that she totally forgot about medicine. She had thought she would work for only a few years until she could earn enough money to go to medical school. Instead, she ended up staying at DuPont until she retired.

At the time Stephanie began working, she was one of the first women research chemists. As a research scientist, she was involved in many projects. One of them was the search for a fiber that could withstand extreme conditions such

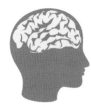

as heat, cold, pressure, or impact. DuPont hoped she would find a lightweight material that could be used in tires.

By dissolving certain chemicals and spinning them into fibers, Stephanie created a fiber that was very stiff and strong. Unlike nylon, it did not break. One of the fibers she discovered would eventually be used to make Kevlar®, a strong material with many purposes.

Stephanie is still amazed at her discovery. She said, "I knew the direction in which to go, but I will tell you this: I never expected to get the properties I did the first time I spun it." Her discovery was, she says, "a case of **serendipity**."

Stephanie was the one who made the first discovery, but many people worked with her to turn her discovery into a useful invention. She said, "Everyone got very excited. We got together a group of people and we decided then there was commercial potential there, and the thing we had to do was find the right fiber for **commercialization**. Everybody got into the act, and it proved to be a very exciting, and sometimes frustrating, time." Some people were in charge of thinking up names for the new material, while others submitted patent applications. Other chemists experimented with new ways to create the fibers and test them. Stephanie said, "It turned out to be a great team effort in the end."

Being an inventor like Stephanie isn't all excitement, though. It takes a lot of hard work. "Every day," Stephanie said, "there are highs and lows, there are times when you think the whole thing will sink because of all the problems that develop." It took ten years between the time Stephanie first stirred that test tube in 1965 to the time bullet-resistant vests made with Kevlar® were available for sale in 1975.

Today, the fibers Stephanie discovered are also used to make boat hulls, cut-resistant gloves, fiber-optic cables, firefighters' suits, fuel hoses, helmets, lumberjacks' suits, parts of airplanes, radial tires, special ropes, pieces of spacecraft, some kinds of bicycles, tennis rackets, canoes, and skis. These fibers are stronger and lighter than steel.

Stephanie has never regretted sticking with chemistry instead of going to medical school. Although she never imagined she would grow up to be an inventor, she said that as a research scientist, "Eventually, you do invent something if you are interested enough and if you work hard enough. I was thrilled when I discovered liquid crystalline solutions." But, she said, it also "takes a certain

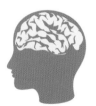

amount of luck, it takes being at the right place at the right time, because you may make an invention but no one may be interested in it at the time."

Stephanie Kwolek is proud that her invention has saved thousands of lives. Her work earned her a place in the National Inventors Hall of Fame and in the National Women's Hall of Fame. She has received over a dozen patents and was awarded the National Medal of Technology, one of the highest honors granted by the President of the United States. Stephanie's life is proof that a love of science can lead you in unexpected directions. You might even change the world with a new invention.

Words to Know

Serendipity: the occurrence of things by chance that work out in a good way.
Commercialization: introduction of a new product for sale.

Find Out More

Stewart, Gail B. *Stephanie Kwolek: Creator of Kevlar*. Detroit, Mich.: KidHaven, 2009.

Famous Women Inventors, "Stephanie Kwolek"
www.women-inventors.com/Stephanie-Kwolek.asp

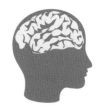

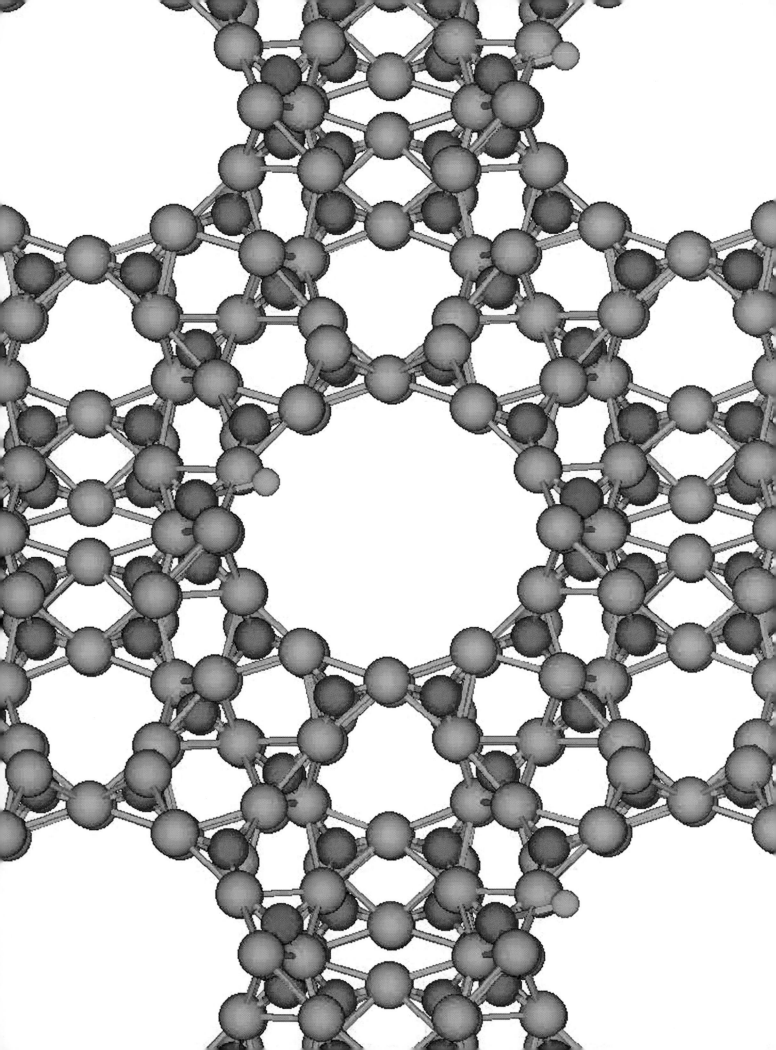

7

Edith Flanigen: New Uses for Zeolites

Like Nystatin, some of the most important inventions are microscopic. This is true of Edith Flanigen's inventions. Despite their small size, however, her inventions affect many aspects of our daily lives, from medical treatments to refrigerators, from laundry soap to jewelry.

Edith was born on January 28, 1929, in Buffalo, New York. When Edith was in high school, she had a chemistry teacher who truly inspired her. Rather than simply lecturing and reading from textbooks, the teacher encouraged Edith and her fellow students to experience firsthand the excitement of chemistry. "She really made it exciting," Edith says. "We did hands-on laboratory work . . . and I think I fell in love with . . . chemistry at that time." This same teacher—a nun—inspired Flanigen's two sisters, who also grew up to become chemists.

Tiny zeolites are used within this huge machinery to clean chemicals from the air.

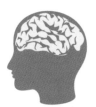

Edith went to college near her hometown of Buffalo and received a bachelor's degree from D'Youville College. In 1952, she earned a master's degree from Syracuse University in **inorganic physical chemistry**. After she had completed her studies, Edith joined Union Carbide Corporation as a research scientist, where she remained for the next forty-two years. She became the first woman corporate research **fellow** there in 1973, and a senior research fellow in 1982.

Edith loved the atmosphere at Union Carbide, and her enthusiasm and expertise had room to grow. She led a team that discovered something called molecular sieve zeolites. This material contains tiny holes that act like the sieve you might use in your kitchen to strain the water off vegetables—except the holes in a zeolite are the size of a molecule. Smaller molecules don't fit through the tiny holes and are absorbed by the zeolite, while larger molecules pass through. Edith and her team discovered more than two dozen different types of zeolites and two hundred ways to build them.

Edith's discoveries are used in many ways. The petroleum industry uses zeolites to change crude oil into gasoline, and also to reduce industrial waste. Zeolites are also used to produce oxygen for portable medical oxygen units. They're used in refrigerators and car air conditioners. And they're being used in laundry detergents, to replace the phosphates that can pollute our environment. Edith has even used zeolites to develop a **synthetic** emerald. She holds more than a hundred patents for her various inventions, all built on her research into zeolites.

Today, Edith is the world's leading authority on these tiny sieves. Her discoveries have not only led to many new uses for zeolites, but they have also opened the door for thousands of other scientists to work in this field.

Edith's work demonstrates the ways that science and invention can interact. Because Edith was a skilled scientist with a deep understanding of chemistry, she was able to make scientific discoveries—and then, her ability to think creatively allowed her to apply those discoveries to solve all sorts of practical, real-life problems. Her work also opened up an entire new area of study, allowing other scientists and inventors to build on her discoveries and ideas.

Edith Flanigen has received many awards throughout her lifetime. In 1991, she became the first woman to receive the Perkin Medal. At the time, this was America's top honor in **applied** chemistry. She is recognized as an out-

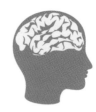

The petrochemical industry uses Edith's zeolites to create gasoline out of crude oil, while reducing waste materials that pollute the atmosphere.

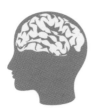

standing woman scientist and was inducted into the National Inventors Hall of Fame in 2004.

Edith wants to help the next generation of scientists as well. She has joined other inventors and educators from across the country to brainstorm ideas for a new math and science school inside the National Inventors Hall of Fame. The group agreed that the environment of the school should be one that focuses on teamwork, creativity, problem solving, experimentation, invention, risk-taking, and "unexpected results." Edith wants others to have a chance to share in the same success she has had. "I'm successful as a scientist," she says, "at least partly because I truly love what I do."

Words to Know

Inorganic physical chemistry: the study of substances that do not contain carbon.

Fellow: a student receiving some money for research.

Synthetic: made by people; often something that imitates a substance made in nature.

Applied: put to practical use.

Find Out More

The American Chemical Society, "Dr. Edith Marie Flanigen"
chicagoacs.net/WCC/flanigen.html

Braun, Sandra. *Incredible Women Inventors*. Toronto, Canada: Second Story Press, 2007.

Invent Now, "HALL OF FAME / inventor profile: Edith Flanigen"
www.invent.org/hall_of_fame/216.html

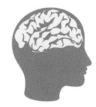

8

Patsy Sherman:
Inventor of
Scotchgard®

S ome inventors look at a problem and try to create a practical way to solve that problem. Other inventors accidentally come across something—and then they think of a way to use it. This is how Patsy Sherman created Scotchgard Stain Repellant. A simple mistake made during a lab experiment led to the invention of a powerful stain repellant that is still used today.

Patsy was born on September 15, 1930, in Minneapolis, Minnesota. When she was in high school, Patsy became very interested in chemistry. But she took a high school **aptitude** test that said she would be most suited to become a housewife. Patsy insisted that she be given the boys' version of the test instead. This time, when she took the test, her results indicated that she should consider dentistry or chemistry as a career. Patsy followed through. She went to college and majored in mathematics and chemistry. After she graduated in 1952 from Gustavus Adolphus College, she went to work for the 3M Corporation as a research scientist. Patsy's job was to come up with new ideas the company could make and sell.

A Changing World

During the time Scotchgard was being developed, very few women worked as scientists or in the business world. When Patsy tried out her inventions' performance at a textile mill, she had to wait for the results outside the building—because women weren't allowed inside! Women like Patsy help change the world, though, and today women have more opportunities than ever before!

While Patsy was working in the lab, one of her assistants dropped a container filled with chemicals, which splashed onto the assistant's shoe. When Patsy and the assistant tried to remove the chemicals, they found that the chemicals, a kind of synthetic **latex**, would not come off. However, the chemicals also prevented anything else from sticking to the shoe.

As Patsy and her coworker Samuel Smith worked with the material, they realized it would make a great stain repellent. When a material was covered with the substance, water and oil couldn't reach the material.

In 1956, the first version of the stain repellant was made and sold. Scotchgard Stain Repellant became a huge success, making millions of dollars for 3M. Patsy holds over a dozen patents for her involvement.

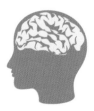

In *Flubber,* Robin Williams played an inventor who stumbled upon an amazing invention. In real life, sometimes whacky accidents can also lead to pretty amazing inventions. Like Patsy, inventors have to be open to the possibilities.

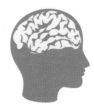

Today's Scotchgard is slightly different from the original design, but it is still based on Patsy's discoveries. It is still one of the most widely used stain repellents in the world, used to protect fabric, furniture, and carpets.

Over time, Patsy became a leader at the 3M Company. In the 1980s, she helped develop and run the technical education department. Her colleagues remember her as someone who was open-minded, **innovative**, and quick-thinking. In her free time, Patsy worked to share her passion for science with young people. She spoke at schools and encouraged students to consider science as a future career.

Patsy understood her importance as a female role model—two of her daughters followed in her footsteps and became scientists as well. One of them even chose become a chemist at the 3M Corporation.

Patsy Sherman died in 2008. During her lifetime, she received many honors for her work as an inventor, and in 2001, she was inducted into the National Inventors Hall of Fame. Patsy was also added to the Minnesota Science & Technology Hall of Fame in 2011.

In 2002, at the bicentennial celebration of the U.S. Patent Office, Patsy called on the world to, "encourage and teach young people to observe, to ask questions when unexpected things happen." She also said that we can all be inventors: "You can teach yourself not to ignore the unanticipated. Just think of all the great inventions that have come through serendipity, such as Alexander Fleming's discovery of penicillin, and just noticing something no one conceived of before."

Words to Know

Aptitude: a natural ability.
Latex: a milky fluid found in some plants.
Innovative: original, creative, introducing new ideas.

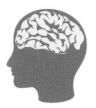

The ultimate stain repellent

Scotchgard is still a popular product used to protect furniture, car seats, and carpets from spills and stains.

Find Out More

Famous Women Inventors, "Patsy Sherman"
www.women-inventors.com/Patsy-Sherman.asp

Invent Now, "HALL OF FAME / inventor profile: Patsy Sherman"
www.invent.org/hall_of_fame/160.html

Thimmesh, Catherine, and Melissa Sweet. *Girls Think of Everything: Stories of Ingenious Inventions by Women.* Boston: Houghton Mifflin, 2000.

9

Opportunities Today for Women Inventors

I n today's age of technology, new inventions bombard us at a faster rate than ever before. You might just be the person who has the next fantastic idea that revolutionizes the way we live our lives. Or you might have a very small but very useful idea that could earn you thousands of dollars in income.

But in the meantime, if you're looking to use your curiosity and creativity in a way that gets you a steady income, you might want to consider a career in science, particularly in research and development.

In the years ahead, women will have more and more job opportunities in science research positions.

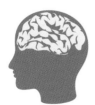

58 WOMEN INVENTORS

Job Outlook

Even though the demand for new research and development is expected to continue growing across all businesses and fields of science, **projected** job growth in the field scientific research and development varies between areas of research. Job growth could also be slowed somewhat by increased technological **efficiency** (which means fewer people are sometimes needed to do the same job) and the rising costs of equipment.

Scientists and engineers, particularly those in the life and medical sciences, are expected to have the largest job growth. **Biotechnology** and **nanotechnology** are also expected to continue growing, driven by the increased demand for new drugs and procedures. Computer-based research-and-design jobs will also grow in number.

The good thing about research-and-development programs is that they usually have lengthy project cycles that keep moving forward even when the

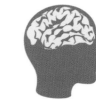

economy slows down. Funding of new research and development, however, especially in industries, can be cut back during periods of economic **recession**. Because the federal government provides about one-fourth of all research-and-development funding, shifts in **policy** also could affect employment opportunities.

Educational and Personality Requirements

Scientific research-and-development jobs need workers who have extensive **postsecondary** education. In 2004, workers who had a bachelor's or higher degree held 68 percent of the jobs in this field.

With only a high school diploma, an associate's degree, or a bachelor's degree, you might be able to start a career in research and development as a technician. Technicians usually work under the direct supervision of a scientist, engineer, or senior technician. They often gradually gain more independence. Continuing on-the-job training is important for using the newest equipment and methods. Some technicians advance to become supervisors responsible for a laboratory or workshop. This could be a good place to get your foot in the door. If you later go back to school for further education, you would then be able to advance to a higher level in this field. Pay will go up as well, if you take that route. With a PhD, you'll likely earn well over $100,000 a year.

For senior scientists and engineers, a master's degree or doctorate is typically necessary. Some fields, particularly in the physical and life sciences, require a PhD even for **entry-level** research positions. In the life sciences, employers increasingly want to hire scientists who have a PhD and have completed a period of academic research, known as a "postdoc," immediately after obtaining a degree. Postdocs may last several years, during which researchers receive low salaries and may have little independence. This opportunity to be on the cutting edge of science and technology could be well worth the extra work, though, and lead to better opportunities in the future.

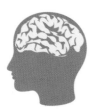

New ideas are waiting to be discovered in the fields of both medicine and computers. In fact, computer technology has increased the speed at which new ideas can be developed. What ideas will you bring to the world?

A PhD and postdoc experience, however, are not enough to guarantee that you'll be successful in this field. You'll need to keep your creative edge if you want to be able to innovate new research and designs. You'll also need to stay up to date and be able to adapt to changes in technologies that may shift interest—and jobs—from one area of research to another.

As a young woman, whether you patent your own private inventions or work for a large company's research-and-development department, you'll have many opportunities in the years ahead. The world will always need your new ideas. And women inventors have already paved the way for you!

Words to Know

Projected: anticipated, forecasted.
Efficiency: how effective something is at getting a job done with the least amount of resources necessary.

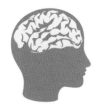

Biotechnology: the study and application of biological processes to industrial purposes.

Nanotechnology: the study and application of how tiny things work.

Economy: a system of resource use.

Recession: a period of temporary economic decline.

Policy: a plan of action adopted by a government or organization.

Postsecondary: referring to education after high school.

Entry level: suitable for a beginner.

Find Out More

Bureau of Labor Statistics, "Careers for Scientists—and Others—in Scientific Research and Development"
www.bls.gov/opub/ooq/2005/summer/art04.pdf

Ideas Uploaded, "20 Successful Inventors offer their Advice to Aspiring Inventors"
ideasuploaded.com/20-successful-inventors-offer-their-advice-to-aspiring-inventors

Tucker, Tom, and Richard Loehle. *Brainstorm! The Stories of Twenty American Kid Inventors.* New York: Farrar, Straus and Giroux, 2008.

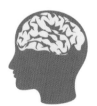

Index

63

About the Author & Consultant

Shaina Indovino is a writer and illustrator living in Nesconset, New York. She graduated from Binghamton University, where she received degrees in sociology and English. She enjoyed the opportunity to apply both her areas of study to a topic that excites her: women in science. She hopes more young women will follow their calling toward what they truly love, whether it be science related or not.

Ann Lee-Karlon, PhD, is the President of the Association for Women in Science (AWIS) in 2014–2016. AWIS is a national non-profit organization dedicated to advancing women in science, technology, engineering, and mathematics. Dr. Lee-Karlon also serves as Senior Vice President at Genentech, a major biotechnology company focused on discovering and developing medicines for serious diseases such as cancer. Dr. Lee-Karlon holds a BS in Bioengineering from the University of California at Berkeley, an MBA from Stanford University, and a PhD in Bioengineering from the University of California at San Diego, where she was a National Science Foundation Graduate Research Fellow. She completed a postdoctoral fellowship at the University College London as an NSF International Research Fellow. Dr. Lee-Karlon holds several U.S. and international patents in vascular and tissue engineering.

Picture Credits

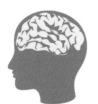